Fish Factories: Ruins of an American Industry

Fish Factories: Ruins of an American Industry

Ruth Formanek, Editor and Photographer

with Essays by H. Bruce Franklin and William Wise

Pogonia Books
New York

Copyright ©2010 Ruth Formanek
An Industry's Ruins
   Copyright ©2010 H. Bruce Franklin
The Early Days of Menhaden Fishing on Long Island
   Copyright ©2010 William Wise

Pogonia Books
170 West End Ave., 27N
New York, NY 10023

ISBN 978-0-9817670-1-7

Printed in Canada

Table of Contents

Acknowledgments

This book will acquaint you with the remnants of a once vibrant and important industry which was based on a fish abundant in the waters of the Atlantic Coast. As over-fishing occurred, the industry disappeared except for one factory in Virginia. H. Bruce Franklin offers a thoughtful history of the menhaden industry, its overfishing and subsequent effects on the environment. William Wise tells the story of the Long Island menhaden fishing and processing industry. The Tuckerton, New Jersey, Historical Society and a Newsletter article by Lori Edmunds were the source of my chapter on the fish factory on Crab Island, locally known as the "Stinkhouse." Ann F. Johnson's book, *Plant Communities of the Napeague Dunes* (1985) introduced me to the existence of the 19th century Long Island fish factories. Natalie Naylor of Hofstra University's Long Island Institute furnished me with old maps and helpful advice. I am grateful for the contributions of the many librarians, historians and others with an interest in our industrial past, especially the East Hampton Free Public Library's Long Island Collection.

As with previous books, I was assisted by a talented team: Anita Gurian was the editor, Martina Mansell, the copy editor, and Naomi Rosenblatt, the book designer.

I have profited from advice and discussions with Elsa Blum, Mike Bottini, Sarah Corbin, Larry Davis, Miriam Forman-Brunell, Alex and David Formanek, Jean Franco, Bruce Franklin, Margery and Ray Franklin, Lewis Friedman, Andrew Gurian, Gisa Indenbaum, Athan and Margot Karras, Lynn Passy, Helen and Chuck Pine, Dwight Primiano, Nancy Sirkis, Paul Stetzer, William Wise, June Zaccone, and many photographers of the Park West Camera Club and Soho Photo Gallery.

Omega Protein, Inc., kindly permitted me access to their recently-acquired factory ruins. All graphic illustrations were found on the Internet and derive from George Brown Goode's book (1880), by courtesy of the National Oceanic and Atmospheric Administration Photo Library (NOAA). I am grateful for permission to use old drawings and photographs from the Freshwater and Marine Image Bank at the University of Washington digital collections. My thanks go to Adobe Photoshop and InDesign (both in CS4 versions) used for the book's layout.

Ruth Formanek

Preface

Little evidence remains of the once flourishing fish factory on tiny Hicks Island, in Napeague Bay, New York. I first saw the rusty machinery parts and a brick stack on the white beach sands. The serene panorama in the golden afternoon light gave no hint of the ruins' earlier functions—to process menhaden (a herring-like fish) into oil and fertilizer. Naturalist Mike Bottini, who took me to see Hicks Island, theorized that construction of the fish factories in the middle of the 19th century had destabilized wooded areas in Napeague Bay. As trees and bushes on the beaches no longer held on to the sand, prevailing winds may have transported sand to the east shore of Napeague Harbor. There, the accumulation of sand may have contributed to the creation of the Walking Dunes, the subject of our 2008 book.[1]

Seeing the fish factory ruins triggered my earlier interest in ruins which began during my childhood years in Bingen on the Rhine. The Rhine and the medieval castles flanking it on both sides were rediscovered and much

Hicks Island, near East Hampton, New York.
Remains of fish factory

discussed during the 19th century romantic movement. Europeans and Americans visited there and many artists, especially British engravers and lithographers, romanticized images of the river and its castles. Richard Wagner wrote operas based on Rhine legends and Victor Hugo described his river voyage.

As a Jewish child I attended school during the first four years of the Hitler regime, when I was exposed to a curriculum which stressed the study of the ruined castles and of the Nibelungen heroes who may have inhabited them. Fortunately in 1938 my family was able to escape persecution and to immigrate to New York City, where I've made my home. Ruins have fascinated me as long as I can remember and I've always sought out places with ruins wherever I was able to travel and photograph.

About 15 years ago I discovered industrial ruins—rusted old cars on Cumberland Island, Georgia, their 1940s bodies penetrated by lush weeds; abandoned boats and shacks about to sink into the sea in Newfoundland, a consequence of the cod-fishing moratorium. Nearer to home, I found the abandoned Hudson River railroad ruins, preserved and embedded in the riverside landscaping.

There are obvious differences between classical and industrial ruins, and Hicks Island is no Acropolis. But fish factory ruins, as all industrial ruins, are important reminders of our past. They tell a story too, albeit a different one from classical mythology or medieval sagas. And they don't remain to be photographed for long—we consider them eyesores, demolish them and build condominiums in their stead.

I was fortunate to find little-known Hicks Island, and began inquiring about the history of its ruins. The Internet led me to Bruce Franklin, a cultural historian at Rutgers University, who was then writing his book, *"The Most Important Fish in the Sea"* (2007).[2] He was able to answer my questions about the menhaden industry and suggested other sites with ruins—Cockrell's Creek, near Reedville, Virginia, and what is locally called the "Stinkhouse," a fish factory ruin on Crab Island, near Tuckerton, New Jersey.

After I had photographed all the fish factory ruins still in existence—at one time there were literally hundreds of plants between Maine and Florida—Bruce Franklin offered to write an essay on the rise and decline of the menhaden-processing industry. William Wise, of the State University of New York (SUNY) Stony Brook, agreed to contribute a chapter on the history of menhaden fishing on Long Island. I wrote the story of Crab Island based on information provided by the Tuckerton, New Jersey, Historical Society.

Our book interweaves two major strands. One is my interest in visual representation, in the photography of industrial ruins. The other strand is Bruce Franklin's cultural-history approach to the rise and decline of a major industry, its overfishing and attendant ecological damage to the waters. The book consists of chapters with different emphases that complement one another.

I took all digital color photographs. Black and white drawings derive from George Brown Goode's book, *The Menhaden Fisheries* (1880), by way of the National Oceanic and Atmospheric Administration (NOAA), and the University of Washington Digital Collections, which also furnished photographs of machinery used in the fish factories.

Leaving Hicks Island. Ruins on top right.

Hicks Island

On Ruins—Classical and Industrial

by Ruth Formanek

Classical (or romantic) ruins, such as the Acropolis in Athens, the Pyramids in Egypt and Chichen Itza in Mexico, have been travel destinations for painters, photographers and tourists, beginning in the early 19th century. Industrial ruins, on the other hand, don't come to mind when we speak of 'ruins,' and are not usually billed as tours by travel bureaus. Remnants of industrial production, industrial ruins attest to capitalist development and its search for profits. Such ruins follow market decisions: when production is moved or stopped altogether, and when older factory buildings are abandoned in favor of newer ones. Industrial ruins are usually viewed as valueless—as trash. Tim Edensor (2005)[3] offers a thoughtful analysis of the characteristics and meanings of ruins, both classical and industrial.

Some industrial ruins are left to decay; in time they become covered and surrounded by weeds while other ruins are first vandalized and burned, then razed and often replaced by new structures. When it becomes too costly to remove ruins, they are often left in place, their quaintness attracting photographers.

Cars belonging to industrialists Andrew and Thomas Carnegie have rusted on their former estate on Cumberland Island, GA, now part of the National Park Service.

11

Industrial ruins are spaces of waste, signifying a vanished prosperity. Such areas become blighted and derelict land is identified with crime and deviancy (Edensor). These meanings, however, apply to urban areas. The fish factories photographed in this book were located outside of cities, at some distance from human habitats, because of their repellent smell. Not the ruined buildings themselves, but their potential to become new reeking fish business prompted Mrs. Alfred I. DuPont to buy up land with burned-out ruins "to ensure that no fish factory would be set up there again."[4]

The Hicks Island ruins rest on a pristine East Hampton bay beach, isolated from the crime and deviancy found among urban industrial ruins, and are host to sea gulls and herons. Urban and rural industrial ruins seem to differ in societal consequences and meanings. Of course, quantity plays a role and fish factory ruins are few in number whereas the Pittsburgh steel ruins, on the other hand, cover large areas.

Industrial ruins and their representation in art differ from those of classical ruins, the most important feature being their relative absence of aesthetic values. History is more relevant in the interpretation of industrial ruins despite their short existence in time—most of them deriving from the 19th and early 20th centuries.

One of the many fish factory ruins on Cockrell's Creek, near Reedville, VA

The Representation of Ruins in Art

The 'Cult of Ruins' began in the 18th century (Huyssen, 2005).[5] Nineteenth-century aesthetic conventions for landscapes with intact buildings or ruins stressed specific features which continue in use today, with the early photographers adding an archeological dimension.

The following is a list of characteristics constituting 19th century aesthetic conventions in regard to ruins that I've gathered from Edensor and from *Antiquity and Photography: Early Views of Ancient Mediterranean Sites,* by Lyons et al. (2005).[6]

The aesthetic conventions of 19th century representations of ruins included:

1. variety and contrast of forms
2. light and dark interplay
3. rough textures
4. busy foregrounds with assorted vegetation, people, animals and boats. Later in the 19th century, railroads often appear in landscapes.

5. Notions of the 'sublime' were added: stormy clouds, as in Turner's paintings of storms at sea, evoking an atmosphere of awe and apprehension of unseen and overpowering magical or natural forces. All suggest a sense of melancholia in the viewer—of a foreboding and uncertain future. Inexorable nature, such as snow-capped mountains, is represented as endangering all things constructed by humans.

Photographers have had an important role in the documentation of ancient ruins—the dawn of photography coinciding with the dawn of archeology. Early photographs were primarily documents of classical ruins, and were frequently mass-produced. After William Fox Talbot's invention of photography (1839), photographers visited the Acropolis in Athens, the pyramids in Egypt, Roman ruins, and many others. Aesthetic conventions were established that were partly due to the limitations imposed by the photographic equipment—the heaviness of cameras and tripods, the difficulty in producing durable photographs, and the need for human beings or animals to stand still during long exposure times.

Note the straight lines and angles in this 1870 frontal view of Acropolis columns by William Stillman which became standard for classical ruins photography.

Preservationists have called for the creation of historical parks in order to preserve the vestiges of our industrial past, such as Lowell National Historical Park in Massachusetts, to interpret the history of America's industrial revolution. In Germany, areas of the industrialized Ruhr (which had furnished war materiel to several German governments) have been turned into a landscape park incorporating structures of the abandoned steel industry.

We have labeled our fish factory photographs according to their location and, where known, their approximate years of operation. To follow Edensor in not labeling photographs suggests that destruction and decay need no identification—that all ruins convey the same depressing message.

We argue that knowledge of history is important, and adds to the evoked emotions. We have therefore labeled our images wherever information was available—much is unfortunately lost. Moreover, if photography is to retain its documentary purpose, identification of images is essential.

The sense of loss, trauma, and melancholia is especially poignant when we are reminded of the fish factories' purpose: Here billions of menhaden were pressed into oil and fertilizer, and overfishing resulted in the decline of the industry as well as lasting damage to the ecology of the waters from which the fish were taken.

Notes

1. Formanek, R., and Bottini, M. *The Walking Dunes: East Hampton's Hidden Treasure* (New York, NY, Pogonia Books, 2008).
2. Franklin, H. B. *The Most Important Fish in the Sea* (Washington, D.C. Island Press, 2007).
3. Edensor, T. *Industrial Ruins: Space, Aesthetics and Materiality* (Oxford, UK. Oxford International Publishers-Berg, 2005).
4. Frye, J. *The Men All Singing: The Story of Menhaden Fishing* (Virginia Beach, VA, The Donning Company, 1978).
5. Huyssen, A. Nostalgia for Ruins (*Grey Room,* Spring 2006, No. 23, p. 6-21, pdf).
6. Lyons, C. L. et al. *Antiquity and Photography: Early Views of Ancient Mediterranean Sites* (Los Angeles, The J. Paul Getty Museum, 2005).

Remnant of a railroad "float bridge" used to load and unload cargo from Hudson River barges. Specialized barges equipped with railroad tracks were floated up to the bridge, where the tracks were aligned, and a locomotive would remove railroad cars from the barge to be delivered in Manhattan. The bridge was used until the 1950s and was preserved when the waterfront was landscaped.

Cockrell's Creek, Reedville, Virginia

All color photographs in this chapter were taken on Cockrell's Creek, near Reedville, Virginia

Chapter 1: An Industry's Ruins

by H. Bruce Franklin*[1]

First you see the birds—gulls and terns wheeling overhead, then swooping down to a wide expanse of water glittering with silver streaks. The sea erupts with frothy splashes, some from the diving birds, others from foot-long fish with deeply forked tails frantically hurling themselves out of the water. More and more birds materialize as if from nowhere. The air rings with their shrill screams. The boiling cloud of birds reveals that a school of menhaden, perhaps numbering in the hundreds of thousands, is being ravaged by a school of bluefish.

---

*H. Bruce Franklin is the John Cotton Dana Professor of English and American Studies at Rutgers University in Newark, NJ.

Attacking from below and behind to slash the menhaden bodies with their powerful jaws, the razor-toothed blues are in a killing frenzy, gorging themselves with the severed backs and bellies of their prey, some killing even when they are too full to eat, some vomiting half digested pieces so they can kill and eat again. Terns skim gracefully over the surface with their pointed bills down, dipping to pluck bits of flesh and entrails from the bloody swirls. Gulls plummet and flop heavily into the water, where a few splash about and squabble noisily over larger morsels. As some lift with their prizes, the squabbles turn aerial and a piece occasionally falls back into the water, starting a new round of shrieking skirmishes. Hovering high above the other birds, a male osprey scans for targets beneath the surface, then suddenly folds its gull-shaped wings and power dives through the aerial tumult, extends its legs and raises its wings high over its head an instant before knifing into the water in a plume of spray, emerges in another plume, and laboriously flaps its four-foot wingspan as it slowly climbs and soars away with a writhing menhaden held headfirst in its talons. Beneath the blues, iridescent weakfish begin

Furnaces generate heat for a Cockrell's Creek plant originally owned by Reedville Oil and Guano Company, then by Haynie Products Company. It was bought by Zapata Haynie Company, changed its name to Zapata, and changed it again to Omega Protein Company.

to circle, snapping at small lumps sinking from the carnage. Farther below, giant but toothless striped bass gobble tumbling heads and other chunks too big for the mouths of the weakfish. From time to time, bass muscle their way up through the blues, swallow whole menhaden alive, and propel themselves back down with their broom-like tails, leaving tell-tale swirls on the surface. On the mud below, crabs scuttle to scavenge on left overs. The panicked school of menhaden desperately races like a single creature, erratically zigging and zagging, diving and surfacing, pursued relentlessly by fish and birds.

Then, as suddenly as it began, the wild scene dissipates. The water becomes surprisingly tranquil, disturbed only by wind and wave. Except for a few gulls lazily circling down and settling on the surface, the birds have disappeared. The menhaden school survives and swims on, its losses dwarfed by plentitude.

But a greater danger than predatory fish lurks nearby:

The birds have attracted a spotter-plane pilot who works for Omega Protein, the corporation that has a monopoly on the menhaden "reduction" industry, which annually converts billions of menhaden into industrial commodities. As the pilot approaches, he sees the school as a neatly defined purplish mass the size of a football field. He radios to a nearby ship, whose 170-foot hull can hold more than a million menhaden. The ship maneuvers close enough to launch two 40-foot-long aluminum boats. The boats share a single purse seine—a net almost a third of a mile long threaded with lines to close it like a purse. The pilot directs the boats as they swing in a wide arc away from each other to deploy the net, surrounding and trapping the entire school. Hydraulic power equipment begins to tighten the seine. As the fish strike the net, they thrash frantically, churning up a wall of white froth that marks the inexorably shrinking circumference. Although each fish weighs only about a pound, there are so many in the net that it may now weigh as much as a blue whale, the largest

animal ever to inhabit our planet. The ship pulls alongside, inserts a giant vacuum tube into the midst of the trapped fish, pumps the menhaden into its refrigerated hold, and soon heads off to unload them at the Omega factory complex in Reedville, Virginia. There they join the hundreds of millions of pounds of other menhaden hauled each year to this tiny town, thus making it in tonnage the second largest fishing port in the United States. Not one of these fish has been caught for people to eat. At Reedville, the fish are boiled and ground into fish meal and oil—hence the term "reduction." The oil from their bodies is pressed out for use in paints, linoleum, health food supplements, lubricants, margarine, soap, insecticide, and lipstick. Their dried-out carcasses are then pulverized, scooped into huge piles, containerized, and shipped out as hog and chickenfeed, pellets for fish farms, and pet food.

These two scenes—the natural and the industrial—have much in common. The first shows nature at its most brutal and efficient. The second shows capitalism as equally brutal and efficient. The big difference is that the forces of nature, though unconscious, are here operating with awe-inspiring creativity and what seems brilliant rationality, while the force of capitalism, though created and operated by human consciousness, is operating with devastating irrationality. For menhaden are the living keystone of the marine ecology of the Atlantic and Gulf coasts, and this single industry, now embodied in this single company, is grinding that keystone into profits for a few individuals, thus tearing down the entire structure of marine life as we know it.

Menhaden: An Integral Part of America's History

Menhaden have always been an integral part of America's history. This was the fish that Native Americans taught the Pilgrims to plant with their corn. This was the fish that made larger scale agriculture viable in the 18th and early 19th century for those farming the rocky soils of New England and Long Island. As the industrial revolution transformed the nation, this was the fish whose oil literally greased the wheels of manufacture, supplanting whale oil as a principal industrial lubricant and additive by the 1870s. In fact, by then the menhaden reduction fishery had become one of America's largest industries. Overall, from the 1860s to the present, catching menhaden has been far and away the nation's largest fishery. In fact, since the end of the Civil War, more menhaden have been caught—not just by numbers but also by weight—than the combined Atlantic and Gulf commercial catch of all other finned fish put together.[2]

All these roles menhaden have played in America's national history are just minor parts of a much larger story, indeed an epic story, of menhaden in America's natural history. For menhaden play dual roles in marine ecology perhaps unmatched anywhere on the planet. And this is why the story of menhaden is the tale of the most important fish in North America.

"The Mission of Menhaden is to be Eaten"
(G. Brown Goode, 1880)

Although those hundreds of billions of menhaden were not caught for us to eat, we do eat them. No, you won't see menhaden in the supermarket seafood counter, but they are there—in the flesh of other fish lying there on the ice. Menhaden are crucial to the diet of most of the predatory fish on our coast, including tuna, bluefish, weakfish, striped bass, swordfish, summer flounder, redfish, and king mackerel. The great 19th-century ichthyologist G. Brown Goode exaggerated only slightly when he declared that people who dine on Atlantic saltwater fish are eating "nothing but menhaden."

Menhaden are also a major component of the diet of many marine birds, including ospreys, gannets, and pelicans, and mammals, including porpoises and toothed whales. Recreational anglers and commercial fishermen know that menhaden are by far the best bait for almost all our marine carnivores. Menhaden scent is such a powerful attractant that it is sold to be sprayed on artificial lures. Commercial lobstermen claim that they cannot make a living without baiting their lobster traps with menhaden. Bluefish, porpoises, and other predators attack in such a frenzy that they sometimes drive whole schools onto beaches. In his monumental volume *A History of Menhaden,* published in 1880, Goode expressed his wonderment at menhaden's role in the natural world: "It is not hard to surmise the menhaden's place in nature; swarming our waters in countless myriads, swimming in closely-packed, unwieldy masses, helpless as flocks of sheep, . . . at the mercy of any enemy, destitute of means of defense or offense, their mission is unmistakably to be eaten."[3]

But Goode was only half right. What he did not fathom was menhaden's other, equally stupendous mission, in marine ecology.

Where did this enormous biomass of menhaden, so crucial to the food web above it, come from? And why do all those marine carnivores go berserk in their mad lust for menhaden? Just as all those saltwater fish are composed largely of menhaden, all those menhaden are composed largely of plankton, including vast amounts of phytoplankton, tiny particles of vegetable matter, mainly algae. For menhaden, eating is just as crucial an ecological mission as being eaten.

Eons before humans arrived in North America, menhaden evolved along the low-lying Atlantic and Gulf coasts, where nutrients flood into estuaries, bays, and wetlands, stimulating potentially overwhelming growth of algae. From this superabundance of algae emerged the superabundance of these fish—and the fish that eat these fish.

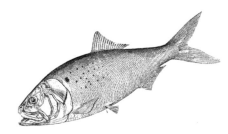

Menhaden, or Brevoortia tyrannos, *a member of the herring family* (from Goode)

The Edwards Company hot-air dryer stopped operating in the early 1940s. Yellow stack (left), built by Morris Fisher Co., provided steam for cooking fish and drying fish scrap (fish meal)

Menhaden's Other Mission: To Filter the Sea

Menhaden are filter feeders that depend on consuming tiny plants and other suspended matter, much of it indigestible or toxic for most other aquatic animals. Dense schools of menhaden, once numbering in the millions, used to pour through these waters, toothless mouths agape, slurping up plankton, cellulose, and just plain detritus like a colossal submarine vacuum cleaner as wide as a city block and as deep as a subway tunnel. Each adult fish can filter an astonishing four gallons of water a minute.[4] To appreciate this feat, turn on your faucet full blast and see if you can get four gallons in a minute. You won't.

These amazing creatures actually digest the cellulose they imbibe, a rare ability for fish and something we can't do. Terrestrial animals that digest cellulose usually have some special mechanism or modality (cows have four stomachs; rabbits and rats eat their own poop).

Menhaden's filter feeding clarifies the water, allowing sunlight to penetrate. This encourages the growth of aquatic plants that release dissolved oxygen while also harboring a host of fish and shellfish.

Even more important, menhaden's filter feeding may also possibly prevent or limit algal blooms. Excess nutrients can make algae grow out of control, and that's what happens when overwhelming quantities of nitrogen and phosphorus flood into our inshore waters from runoff fed by paved surfaces, roofs, detergent-laden wastewater, over-fertilized golf courses and suburban lawns, and industrial poultry and pig farms. These devastating blooms of algae, including red tide and brown tide, cause massive fish kills, then sink in thick carpets to the bottom, where they smother plants and shellfish, suck dissolved oxygen from the water, and leave vast dead zones that expand year by year.

Marine biologist Sara Gottlieb compares menhaden's role with the human liver's: "Just as your body needs its liver to filter out toxins, ecosystems also need those

27

natural filters." Overfishing menhaden, she says, "is just like removing your liver."[5]

Menhaden's two great missions—eating and being eaten—are tightly interwoven in the great web of marine ecology. I asked why do all these marine fish and birds and mammals go berserk in their obsessive appetite to gorge on menhaden. Just like us, all those marine carnivores have to have Omega-3 fatty acids. These are essential nutrients. And just like us, all those marine carnivores are incapable of synthesizing their own. We can get Omega-3 by eating certain grains, nuts, and, best of all, oily ocean fish. Where can ocean fish get their Omega-3? Only by eating other fish that somewhere along the food web had eaten vegetable matter, mainly algae, the best source of Omega-3. Menhaden, the champion consumers of algae, are therefore their most direct and efficient source of Omega-3. To us, menhaden are unappetizing because they stink with the oils derived partly from algae. This stench is precisely what attracts all those marine carnivores, whose bodies have evolved to tell them that bite for bite they are going to get more

of those precious lipids from menhaden than from anything else they can possibly eat.

Both of the crucial ecological functions of menhaden are now threatened by the ravages of unrestrained industrial fishing. By the end of the 20th century, the population and range of Atlantic menhaden had virtually collapsed. The estimated numbers of sexually mature adult fish had crashed to less than 13 percent of what it had been just four decades earlier.[6] Northern New England had once been the scene of the largest menhaden fishery. During the fall migration, menhaden formed a solid body, with the vanguard reaching Cape Cod before the rear guard had left Maine. Today it is rare to see any schools of adult menhaden north of Cape Cod. Menhaden managed to survive centuries of relentless natural and human predation. But now there are ominous signs that we may have pushed our most important fish to the brink of an ecological catastrophe.

Try pots were used to boil whale oil, later menhaden oil (from Goode)

Early Use of Menhaden in Farming

The name "menhaden" comes from the Narragansett Indians' name *munnawhatteaûg*, which means "he enriches the land."[7] What they meant by that was simple: used in modest subsistence farming, the fish bequeathed its rich nutrients to the soil. The earliest 17th-century colonists used menhaden Indian style, burying the fish hill by hill with their seed corn. But when draft animals such as oxen were transported from England, farmers could plow large fields, so they began growing the Indian corn not as a subsistence crop but as a market commodity. The European plow agriculture suitable for grains such as wheat, rye, and barley was now being used on a crop the Indians had developed for cultivation with a hoe. Because of its high profits, corn lured farmers into monoculture, unlike the Indians' ecologically sound methods of mixing plants, such as using corn stalks as bean poles for legumes that hold nitrogen in the soil. Corn demands an extremely high supply of nutrients, especially nitrogen to stimulate fast growth of the lush stalks as well as phosphorus and potassium to make the stalks and roots firm enough to hold the cobs. One way the Indians met this need was by planting the corn in new grounds, which they could do simply by moving the farm, a solution unavailable in a European system based on private ownership of the land.

By the late 18th century, many of the farms in New England and Long Island were suffering from soil exhaustion. Farmers along the shores of Long Island, Connecticut, and Rhode Island started becoming part-time menhaden fishermen. When the fish were spotted, farmers rushed to their boats and rowed out to trap the school between their seine and the shore. The seine was secured to a massive cast-iron black capstan on the beach, where a lumbering horse trod around and around, turning the capstan and thus pulling the net with its thrashing masses of fish, sometimes weighing fifty tons or more, toward the beach.[9] As the dying menhaden piled up on the sand, other farmers came to purchase some of this cheap manure and truck it back in their horse-driven wagons for their own fields.[10]

Then came the Civil War and its aftermath, which accelerated America's transformation from a rural, agricultural society into an urban industrial society, with a larger and larger population needed to be fed. There were now demands for enormous quantities of both fertilizer for farms and oils for industrial processes and products. Hence the birth of the menhaden reduction industry.

Whaling as the First Industrialized Fishery

The first industry in which the United States became the undisputed global leader was whaling. By 1846, almost three-fourths of the whale ships in the world were American. In a nation that was industrializing at a frenzied pace, whale oil flowed like petroleum today into illumination, lubrication, and a multitude of manufactured products. And baleen (the brush-like filter in the mouths of planktivore whales) was "the plastic of its age," used in everything from corset stays to buggy whips.[11] Yet within three decades, the whale industry would be dwarfed by the menhaden industry. By 1874, the production of menhaden oil, which was rising, was already 50 percent greater than the production of whale oil, which was declining.[12] By 1876, half a billion menhaden were being processed each year in a hundred factories strung up and down the eastern seaboard.[13] By 1880, the number of menhaden ships was almost triple the number of whale ships.[14] In *Moby-Dick; Or, The Whale,* published in 1851 during the peak decade of the whaling industry, Herman Melville wrote: "[N]owhere in all America will you find more patrician-like houses; parks and gardens more opulent, than in New Bedford. Whence came they?…Yes; all these brave houses and flowery gardens…were harpooned and dragged up hither from the bottom of the sea."[15] Twelve years later, a New Bedford newspaper would be drooling about "the almost fabulous profits" being made elsewhere in the "Menhaden fishery," and hoping that New Bedford would be able to catapult into the booming new business.[16] By 1884, owners of menhaden companies would be "the richest to be found in the provincial towns of New-England and on Long Island," constituting, as the *New York Times* put it, a new "aristocracy of the country."[17] This world-famous whaling port of New Bedford, which indeed then did have the highest per capita

The Viking (only its hull is visible) was built in 1872 and presumably used for menhaden fishing. Its last captain was William F. Haynie. The Viking was abandoned near Reedville, VA, in 1916.

income in the nation, would soon yield this distinction to Reedville, a town on isolated Cockrell's Creek in Virginia's Northern Neck, founded as a menhaden port by a Yankee sea captain Elijah Reed, who sailed into the creek in 1868 with two schooners and some menhaden reduction equipment. The opulent Victorian mansions that still line Reedville's streets, like the town itself, were all built by the billions of menhaden hauled up from the sea and the waters of the Chesapeake.[18]

Not since the nineteenth century has whaling been a significant American industry, while menhaden is still the nation's largest fishery in numbers of fish caught. Nineteenth-century American whaling was also the first truly industrialized fishery. It industrialized because of the rising demand for industrial oil, coupled with the astonishingly long voyages of the typical whaler. Half the Yankee ships sailing from New Bedford fished in the Pacific Ocean, necessitating many months of travel to and fro, as well as years of hunting on a single voyage. This meant that the dead whales had to be butchered alongside and onboard the ships, passed through the in-

dustrial process known as "trying out," and then stored as barrels of oil or baleen. To do that, the factory that manufactured the oil had to be brought on board. Thus the typical Yankee whale ship became a floating factory and its crew became factory workers. At the center of that floating factory was the "try works."

Moby-Dick is, among many other things, the first great American novel set largely inside a factory and describing in precise detail the tools, machinery, and methods of industrial labor. Its preeminent factory scene is the "Try-Works" (chapter 96), which begins with a description of the massive try-works, "planted between the foremast and mainmast, the most roomy part of the deck.....The timbers beneath are of a peculiar strength, fitted to sustain the weight of an almost solid mass of brick and mortar, some ten feet by eight square, and five in height." Inside are the two "great try-pots,.....each of several barrels' capacity." Directly underneath the pots are "the two iron mouths of the furnaces":

Standard Products factory at Fairport, near Reedville, Virginia

These mouths are fitted with heavy doors of iron. The intense heat of the fire is prevented from communicating itself to the deck, by means of a shallow reservoir extending under the entire inclosed surface of the works. By a tunnel inserted at the rear, this reservoir is kept replenished with water as fast as it evaporates.

The night after killing a sperm whale, cutting into the body, and hauling the huge strips of blubber aboard, the crew fires the Pequod's furnaces. As the harpooners feed the blubber into the try pots, the ship, plunging into "the wild ocean darkness," belching smoke and stench, lit by the red fires of its furnaces, and sloshing with boiling whale oil, becomes at once an inferno, an hallucinogenic vision of hell, a symbol of its mad captain's quest for revenge against nature, and a realistic representation of the factories converting the bodies of animals and the labor of people into dollars.

The very year that *Moby-Dick* was published, industrial methods were being developed simultaneously in Maine, Connecticut, and New York for trying out oil from menhaden. In the prominent whaling port of Greenport on the eastern end of Long Island, whal-

ers' try pots were actually being used to separate the oil from menhaden bodies and a successful factory was beginning operations. By 1867, the menhaden fishery had entirely eclipsed the whale fishery in Greenport, around which clustered twenty menhaden factories processing the teeming schools of Peconic Bay and Gardiner's Bay.[19] The Long Island Railroad, which had previously been extended to Greenport in order to transport whale products, now instead filled its trains with menhaden products.

Why did the whale fishery collapse and the menhaden fishery arise from its ruins? Several factors converged to hurl the whale industry down from its peak in the 1850s. Up to this time, whale oil was a primary source of illumination, but this role was being rapidly usurped by new sources of lighting, including kerosene derived from coal and, more important, natural gas, which was soon flowing through networks of pipes to inaugurate the gaslight epoch of late nineteenth-century urban America. Whale oil's second major role, lubrication, was also threatened by kerosene and soon, far more decisively, by petroleum. In 1859, in Pennsylvania, came that event

still rocking the world: oil gushing from the first commercially viable well. Whale oil's other main uses, as a constituent of industrial processes like tanning, and a component of such industrial products as paints, soaps, and cosmetics, would soon have a cheaper substitute—menhaden oil, which was also even a cheaper lubricant than petroleum.

The Decline of Whaling and the Rise of the Menhaden-Reduction Industry

The Civil War was a disaster for whaling and a golden opportunity for the menhaden reduction industry. Forty-six slow-sailing whale ships were captured or destroyed by modern Confederate cruisers such as the *Alabama*, *Florida*, and *Shenandoah* (all built in England and crewed mainly by British seamen). Another forty, whose owners were now eager to get out of the whaling business, were bought by the federal government, filled with stones, and sunk in a futile attempt to block southern ports.[20] With whale oil scarce and war industries consuming more and more oils, demand and prices for menhaden oil soared.[21] In the wake of the war, an 1867 *Scientific American* article titled "The Menhaden Oil Mania" could refer to this as "a mania second only to the petroleum excitement." [22]

By 1871, *Scientific American* was lamenting the fate of Sag Harbor, Long Island, "once one of the largest and most important of the whaling towns," which "now does almost no business in that line" because its place has been taken by the menhaden industry which "has grown into enormous proportions, and is immensely profitable."[23] Later that year, famed New York City artist Gilbert Burling visited the Long Island factories, sailed with the menhaden fishermen, and then wrote a fascinating account, illustrated with thirteen of his own fine drawings, for *Appleton's Journal*. He began with these revealing words:

Not hundreds of feet below the surface of the soil, shut up in crevices of rocks, but in the surrounding waters, are found the oil-supplies of Long Island…[A] few years ago, the eastern end of it was built up by adventurous whalemen, who then established the principal villages of Sag Harbor, Greenport, and Orient. Their occupation gone with the almost extinct whales, these hardy fishermen left to their sons a gentler livelihood, gained by netting a finny prey they would have despised—for the moss-bunker, menhaden, or bony fish, is a little creature of something near a pound only in weight—to the great whale, what a fly is to an ox.[24]

The postwar menhaden reduction industry had obvious competitive advantages over whaling. Why chase a decimated whale population halfway around the globe when what was called "the miniature whale" was cramming the whole coast?[25] In a single week a menhaden vessel might be able to bring in as much oil as a whaler on a multiyear voyage—and without the frightful risks of whaling. After all, of 787 whale ships in the New Bedford fleet during its peak years, 272 were lost on whaling voyages.[26] Moreover, except for the extracted oil and baleen from the planktivores, the meat and the rest of the whales' bodies were discarded as valueless.[27] But the dried-out bodies of the bunkers—stripped of the oil that corrupted their value as fertilizer, then dried, pulverized, and conveniently packaged for transport and storage—were thus transformed into further wealth for the owners of the menhaden factories.

As soon as those first factories began operations in the 1850s, they were immediately hailed as rescuers of America's depleted soils and liberators from dependency on Peruvian guano. Desperate for nitrogen and phosphorus, America's farmers had been forced to import guano all the way from Peru, and these droppings of sea birds were quite pricey by the time they were shipped around Cape Horn, unloaded in U.S. ports, and transshipped to the farms. The 1855 article "Manure from the Sea," printed in both the *Maine Farmer* and the *Southern Planter*, enthused about the ocean as "a vast reservoir" from which "may be taken an almost unlimited supply of material, by which to replenish the exhausted fertility of the earth."[28] In "Artificial Guano from the Sea," *The Cultivator* recognized that "millions of fish can be obtained at a trifling cost" and trusted that this "artificial fish-manure.....can be manufactured so cheap as to drive the foreign guano from the market."[29]

Just as menhaden oil was pouring into American industry, menhaden "guano" or "scrap" was feeding American agriculture. Trainloads of this "artificial fish-manure" were soon streaming from the ports and factories of New England, Long Island, and New Jersey to inland states and, briefly before the Civil War, to the South. But the southern fishery itself was about to explode, thanks to the Chesapeake Bay and the rich waters off the coast of Virginia and North Carolina, where menhaden could be hunted all year round.

Within months of the end of the Civil War in 1865, New Englanders in the menhaden business were rushing to check out the Chesapeake for exploitation. There, according to G. Brown Goode, they found menhaden "so thick that for 25 miles along the shore there was a solid flip-flap of the northward-swimming fish." These Yankee businessmen got so carried away that "one enthusiastic member of the party jumped into the water and with a dip-net threw bushels of fish upon the beach."[30] In December of that year, one of the thriving menhaden industrialists of Greenport dispatched his steamer *Ranger* to fish the Chesapeake. Emulating the whale ships, the *Ranger* was a factory ship fully equipped with the furnaces, boilers, and the rest of the industrial apparatus necessary to process the menhaden and store the products. It took only eleven days for the *Ranger* to fill to capacity (in stunning contrast to a typical whaling voyage).[31] To fish this far from a home port, a ship would need to be a floating factory because otherwise the menhaden would rot before they could be processed. But factory ships were not the wave of the future, and the short-lived experiments with them merely showed a failure to think outside the whale-fishery box. Instead of sending ships on long voyages to hunt an elusive quarry, it made more sense to berth the ships and set up the factories right next to where the quarry conveniently packed themselves.

Menhaden-Processing Factories Pollute the Environment

Although nineteenth-century whaling was an industrialized fishery, the post-Civil-War menhaden fishery was a far more blatant and integrated component of an industrialized society. Hundreds of menhaden factories belched their black smoke and stench along the nation's coast, not, like Melville's ship, somewhere out in the middle of the Pacific Ocean. Unlike crewmen on a whale ship, there was nothing that could even be viewed as romantic or adventurous about the grueling lives of the workers who labored long hours inside these reeking factories, their bodies permeated by the stink of cooked and ground bunker. One of the worst fates for Jurgis, the protagonist of Upton Sinclair's 1906 naturalist novel *The Jungle*, is having to work in a fertilizer plant amid the Chicago stockyards and slaughterhouses, making him stink so bad that nobody can tolerate being near him. An 1879 visitor to a "fish guano" factory wonders "how persons stand" the smell "who have to work among it," and notes that anyone who works there a week carries so much of its "perfume" with him that "he is debarred from all social relations with the outside world." Even when guano was put outside to dry, "the windows of a church two miles away had to be closed."[32]

The menhaden factories were such awful polluters that they were often "driven away as a public nuisance" from settled areas and forced to relocate in some "desolate spot" like Promised Land out toward the eastern tip of Long Island, as described in "The Menhaden Fishery and Factories" in *Lippincott's Magazine of Popular Literature and Science:* "Its salient features are six great brown-and-red factories, with black chimneys…and long docks thrust out like antennae into the waters of the bay. About these are grouped the frame dwellings that shelter the workers and their families"[33]

What kinds of working conditions and pay would lead owners to bring black workers from the south, especially with a large immigrant labor force available in nearby New York City? The author doesn't say, even when he finds the same labor force of "sleek Virginia negroes" elsewhere in his tour of the menhaden factories lining both the north and south shores of Long Island as well as Connecticut. On Barren Island, located right on the edge of New York Harbor, he finds "three hundred

The bricks are all that's left of the first steam fish factory on Cockrell's Creek

Another remnant of an early fish factory

sleek and oily negroes…spreading and raking on wide board platforms the shredded remnants of what yesterday was darting in life and beauty through the water."[34]

The steamship, that terrible new weapon that marked the doom of the sail ship during the Civil War, became soon after the war an equally ominous weapon when aimed at those teeming masses of fish that had once seemed inexhaustible. No fish or school of fish could swim fast enough or far enough to escape the range of the modern fishing vessels being fabricated in the post-war shipyards.

The menhaden reduction industry was the vanguard of the overall industrialization of fisheries in post-Civil War America. By 1874, an article in the *New York Times* could boast that "the methods by which fish are captured in the United States are superior to those in use in all other countries," thanks to "what may be called industrial fishing."[35] With the menhaden industry leading the way, American industrial fishing was already on course toward self destruction as it devastated the marine environment.

In the decade after the Civil War, nowhere did the Gold Rush frenzy explode greater than in Maine. Between 1866 and 1876, more than twenty menhaden factories suddenly materialized on these rocky shores. A flotilla of 300 vessels, including dozens of mass-produced steamships, were supplying the factories' insatiable appetite for Maine "pogies."[36]

Overfishing Leads to Collapse of the Menhaden Factories

As the menhaden steamships spread their huge purse seines and hauled millions of menhaden back to their factories for industrial processing, Maine's other commercial fishermen suddenly found their livelihood threatened. The fish they hunted were disappearing because the food these fish needed were disappearing into the menhaden factories. The commercial fishermen revolted, rioting in the towns of Bristol and Bremen, and burning down at least one menhaden factory. Then they turned in their desperation to the Maine legislature to demand the outlawing of the reduction industry. The manufacturers responded that menhaden are "practically inexhaustible." After a long fight, the fishermen won. In 1879, Maine became the first state to ban the menhaden reduction industry from its waters.

But it was too late. The menhaden were gone. Marine scientists claimed this was just a cyclical event, probably due to water temperature, and predicted that the men-haden would soon return. They were wrong. What had happened to those myriads of menhaden in Maine waters, where they had been so wondrously abundant? Nine years later, the *New York Times* was still reporting that nobody had "been able to discover why the masses of [menhaden] which once lined the rugged shores of Maine…no longer go there…[N]ow the factories there are rotting down."[37] Marine scientists were confounded because they were still following the leadership of Thomas Henry Huxley, who wrote in 1883: "…all the great sea fisheries, are inexhaustible;…nothing we do seriously affects the number of the fish. And any attempt to regulate these fisheries seems consequently … to be useless."[38]

Similar stories repeated down the Atlantic coast, as the reduction industry caused crash after crash of the menhaden population and thus self-destructed. The collapse swallowed up the southern New England fishery, including the 13 factories that had ringed Narragansett Bay, along with the reduction industry that had transformed both the economy and marine ecology of Long Island and coastal New Jersey. State after state followed

Maine's example, outlawing the industry after most of the damage had been done. The fierce struggles initiated by Maine's commercial fishermen against the reduction industry have raged continually for more than a century and a quarter, with recreational anglers and environmentalists today pitted against the Omega Protein monopoly in a life and death struggle over the environment.

While the battle was nearing its climax in Maine, physical confrontations were erupting in the rich fishing waters of New Jersey. Sometimes the battles verged on actual warfare. In 1877, New Jersey fishermen and recreational anglers threatened to procure cannons and "fire on the marauding steamers."[39] In 1882, the legislature passed a bill outlawing the reduction industry, only to have it vetoed by the governor. The fight to get the menhaden reduction vessels out of New Jersey waters would go on throughout the 20th century.[40] Finally in 2001, the legislature passed and the governor signed a bill just like the one vetoed back in 1882, making New Jersey the twelfth Atlantic state to ban the industry.

A Revolution in American Cultural Thought: The Birth of Ecological Consciousness

The natural history of this fish is breathtaking and its national history in America, virtually unknown, is astonishing. Equally amazing is its cultural history. It's not too often that one finds a radical shift in cultural consciousness occurring in the blink of an historical eye. Yet in a period of about a dozen years, the fight over menhaden was generating the concept of the interdependence of species and forcing this concept into public culture, forming the core of an ecological consciousness with a new vision of human relations to the life of the sea. Food chain, web of life, ecology—these everyday twenty-first century ideas grew from this struggle.

By forcing people to rethink predator-prey relations, menhaden demanded a revolution in American cultural thought. Although other humans have eaten almost every kind of terrestrial animal and insect, the land animals generally eaten in Europe and America are not predators. So we raise sheep, cattle, pigs, chickens, ducks, geese, and turkeys for us to eat, and we protect them against the other animals that want to eat them, such as wolves, foxes, mountain lions, coyotes, raccoons, and possums. From the colonists on, the attitude toward terrestrial predators was simple: Kill them! The colonists had a massive—and fairly successful—program aimed at exterminating wolves.[41] Protecting prey in order to preserve predators would seem like protecting sheep in order to preserve wolves.

Although the animals at the meat counter are mostly terrestrial prey species, the animals at the fish counter are mostly marine predators. When it comes to fish from the sea, we Americans generally eat carnivores. Most of our food and game fish are devourers of flesh and savage predators of other fish.[42] So protecting menhaden to guarantee a good supply of bluefish at the fish market was something like protecting chickens to guarantee a good supply of foxes at the meat market. But if predators depend on prey, and we value the predators—well, you see where that leads: to that radical notion of the interdependence of species. Were the purse-seiners indeed taking away the fish that the other fish needed to eat? Was this a major cause of the obvious decline of America's food fish? Were the menhaden "monopolists" and "capitalists" menacing the livelihood of fishermen? Arguments and counter-arguments reverberated in the only public media of the period, newspapers and magazines. This fierce fight for public opinion succeeded in making environmental questions part of popular discourse and consciousness.

In 1882, in the early stages of the debate, the *New York Times* contemptuously dismissed menhaden as this "mongrel fish" and scoffed at "that relationship which one creature is supposed to bear to another." The *Times* ridiculed the claim that "the enormous takes" of menhaden "deprive edible fish of their food." The *Times* attempted to refute such a silly notion by parroting the inexhaustibility argument of Thomas Henry Huxley and other scientists: "It has been shown over and over again that man's take of the sea fishes is utterly insignificant when the whole bulk of the fish is considered. Preda-

Two boats from the old menhaden fleet left at dockside after Ampro Fisheries closed their operation. Built in 1945 for the U.S.Navy, they were converted to fishing boats. 49

ceous fish and birds, all the natural enemies of the fish, destroy more perhaps in a single hour than man captures in the year."[43] The *Times* writers had not yet witnessed the full destructive potential of human technology.

By the early 1890s, consciousness had dramatically shifted. In 1893, just eleven years after pooh-poohing the concept of the interdependence of species, the *New York Times* published a major article with headlines spelling out its new position: "Food for Predatory Fish: Menhaden, The Ocean's Vast Animal Pasturage. The Common Fodder That Affords Subsistence to All the Game Species of the Sea Gradually Decreasing—Necessity of Protecting [Menhaden] in Order to Preserve the Food Fish." Here appeared a true ecological vision of menhaden and the sea: "Like the grasses of the far-rolling prairie are they in number, and like them they transmute the raw material of the soil" into food "for a multitude of other forms of life."

Although ecological, this vision of menhaden was only partial and certainly not holistic. Repeating Goode's 1880 formulation, it still saw only half of the whole:

"The menhaden is to be considered as mere fodder; his mission is to be eaten; he exists only for others." A touch of wonder comes from sensing the scale of this mission: "The need therefore of its existence in swarming myriads is readily appreciated, and renders creditable statements that otherwise would seem too marvelous for belief. In the opinion of competent authorities the number of menhaden annually destroyed by other fish along our coast exceeds in weight that of the entire human population of the globe, and yet the surviving multitude is impressive in its vastness." The *Times* then stated as fact that menhaden "render subsistence to every predatory fish that inhabits its waters."

Half a century later, the ecological consciousness of the 1890s was swept away by the tide of victory culture that deluged America in the 1940s. The Second World War had ended in what seemed a triumph of American technological might, and the nation looked forward to an epoch when the genie of technology would continue to grant the country invincibility and boundless prosperity. Indeed there were no limits for the menhaden reduction industry, which by then was based in coastal North

Carolina and the Chesapeake. Menhaden corporations scooped up "surplus" warships, almost brand-new minesweepers and submarine chasers at negligible cost. These rugged vessels had been designed for rough ocean seas and were already equipped with state-of-the-art communications equipment. Once retrofitted for bunker fishing, the weapons of war could be hurled at the huge offshore schools that had so far withstood three quarters of a century of assaults from the industry. Now all that was needed was a modern method to locate these schools. The obvious solution was the weapon that had supposedly won the war: the airplane. Locating the schools no longer depended upon the sharp vision of a lookout in the crow's-nest of a ship wallowing amid the ocean's waves. A spotter plane, canvassing huge areas at relatively high speeds, could quickly spy the schools. For the first time, menhaden's oceanic spawning was seriously endangered.

Unrestrained Slaughter of Menhaden

I was fortunate to find the man who revolutionized the menhaden industry, its first spotter pilot, Hall Watters.

Watters, who had been a youthful fighter pilot during World War II, pioneered the methods still used in the fishery. Guided by Watters, the ships, designed for trans-Atlantic patrols, were able to net schools as far out as fifty miles, some with so many egg-filled females that the nets, he said, "would be all slimy from the roe."

Watters believed that "1960 was really the turning point" in the one-sided war against the fish. He vividly remembered that year spotting a school about "five city blocks in diameter" and "dragging mud in 125 feet of water," that is, solid all the way from the surface down to the seabed. "I couldn't believe **they could destroy a** school that size," he told me, but boats did annihilate the entire school. After 1960, he observed the schools getting smaller and smaller.

The popular media were expressing boundless enthusiasm for this unrestrained slaughter. A 1949 article in *National Geographic* boasted that "more menhaden have been taken from American waters than any other species" and enthused to its readers about how "Uncle Sam's largest commercial fishery" enriched their lives:

51

Standard Products Factory

Renovated remnants of fish factories grace a suburban garden in Ditchley, Virginia.

The soap in your kitchen and bathroom is apt to contain menhaden oil. The linoleum on your kitchen or office floor, the varnish and paint that decorate the furniture and walls in your home, and your waterproof garments may have been made with the oil. Steel manufacturers use the oil in tempering their product.[44]

LIFE magazine's 1951 treatment, titled "Biggest Ocean Harvest: The lowly menhaden, top U.S. commercial fish, is hunted by scientifically equipped task force," expressed the ethos of the period by focusing on the electrifying wonders of science and technology. To reap the "rich marine harvest" of this "most-caught fish in American waters," the "menhaden men" use the very latest in technology: airplanes, "the radio telephone," and "their most important scientific acquisition," the Bendix "electronic fish finder," adapted directly from wartime sonar. The victories over the menhaden, while of course not as spectacular or devastating as the thousand-plane bomber raids that thrilled the nation during the actual war, were in their own quiet way certainly formidable—and ominous for the environment.

In the year 2000, still living in his native North Carolina town of Wilmington at the age of 75, Hall Watters summed up the story cogently: "The industry overfished their own fishery and they destroyed it themselves. And they're still at it." Referring to himself and the other spotter pilots, he said, "We're the worst culprits." "If you took the airplanes away from the fleet," he said, "the fish would come back but the company would go out of business because they couldn't find the fish."

By the time Hall Watters used the word "company" in the year 2000, he meant just one company because by then that's about all that was left. The familiar pattern of overfishing, population collapse, and industry consolidation had repeated itself with a vengeance along the entire Atlantic seaboard and was then ravaging the Gulf.

As the menhaden population crashed, numerous small and medium-sized companies went bankrupt or were bought out by bigger companies. The corporate consolidation continued relentlessly. One by one, every com pany in the Atlantic was gobbled up by Zapata, a corporation originally founded in 1953 by George H. W. Bush as an oil and gas wildcatter. In the 1990s, Zapata turned itself into Omega Protein—a jazzy new name more fit for a health-food company—which now has a virtually total monopoly on the menhaden reduction industry.

Back in the 1980s, the industry put out a film claiming that menhaden are an unlimited self-sustaining natural resource. The film is titled *America's Menhaden Industry: A Success Story.* Every company mentioned in the film is now out of business. The factory shown in the film as a model of successful enterprise can be glimpsed in Ruth Formanek's haunting pictures of ruins along Cockrell's Creek. Indeed, her photographs in this volume are a wonderfully eloquent vision of the history of the menhaden reduction industry.

Disintegrating fish factories and rotting bunker vessels are scattered along the East coast of the United States, grim remains today of the industry that wiped out most of the Atlantic menhaden. These are not tourist attractions like the Monterey Bay Aquarium and the restaurants in the old factories of what used to be Cannery Row in Monterey, memorials to the industry that destroyed itself along with most of California's sardines. Some, though, are still used as local landmarks. Fishing maps of New Jersey's Little Egg Harbor and Great Bay, for example, mark the site of a crumbling menhaden factory—prominently labeled "Stinkhouse." And there is the Reedville Fishermen's Museum, located on Main Street in Reedville on Cockrell's Creek.

Down Cockrell's Creek from the museum is all that is left of the once vast industry that hunted Atlantic menhaden from Maine to Florida: Omega Protein's East Coast factory complex, airfield, and eleven-ship fleet. Across the creek from Omega's plant are rusting hulks of various vintages and the smokestack of an abandoned factory, leftovers from competitors bought out by Omega. Further up the creek are more crumbling menhaden factories, trees pushing up through their vine-covered ruins. In the heyday of the industry, more than sixty steamers brought their daily menhaden hauls to eight factories clustered along this remote little tributary of the mighty Chesapeake. [46]

The great oceanic schools are also gone. By 2005, almost eighty percent of Omega's catch was coming out of the Virginia waters of the Chesapeake. And the Chesapeake itself is dying. Stripped of its menhaden, the Bay is choked by ever-expanding dead zones caused by algal blooms. Deprived of their essential menhaden diet, seventy percent of the Bay's resident striped bass by 2007 were infected with a kind of fish tuberculosis caused by malnutrition.

A Future for the Menhaden?

But menhaden are an amazingly fecund species. Given a chance, they could come back and help us bring back much of what we have lost. Saving the whales is a great cause. But for the Atlantic coast, saving menhaden is a more crucial cause.

And what if we do succeed in saving and restoring menhaden? Imagine that scene with which I opened this essay expanding more and more until it fills the waters of the Atlantic coast—as it did until the middle of the nineteenth century. Let us imagine, if we can, recovering that great bounty of nature that we have almost entirely destroyed, that fabulous marine environment that awed the first European voyagers to this continent. A fitting accompaniment to that scene might then be Ruth Formanek's photographs of the ruins of the very last menhaden factory, a reminder of human greed and folly.

Notes

1. Some portions of this chapter appeared earlier in my book, *The Most Important Fish in the Sea* (Washington, D.C.: Island Press, 2007, 2008), reprinted here by permission of Island Press. Copyright 2007 by H. Bruce Franklin; all rights reserved.
2. Take for example some of the statistical compilations provided by the U.S. National Oceanic and Atmospheric Administration (NOAA) in its annual Fisheries of the United States. According to the average provided by NOAA for 1982-1987, the annual combined haul of all other finned species was 2.1 billion pounds while the menhaden haul was 2.75 billion pounds. For previous years, NOAA compiled tables of the total catch for each of the "principal species." In 1955, the combined catch of all the other principal species was 975 million pounds, while the menhaden catch

was 1.7 billion pounds; in 1965, the catch of the other principal species was 1.4 billion pounds, while the menhaden catch was 1.8 billion pounds; in 1975, the other principal species catch was 1.1 billion pounds, menhaden 1.8 billion pounds. Since menhaden are small and the other principal species included such large fish as tuna, salmon, and cod, the number of menhaden caught is many times the combined totals of the other fish.

3. G. Brown Goode, *A History of the Menhaden* (New York: Orange Judd, 1880), pp. 109-110.

4. Sara J. Gottlieb, Ecological Role of Atlantic Menhaden *(Brevoortia Tyrannus)* in Chesapeake Bay and Implications for Management of the Fishery (University of Maryland, College Park: Master's Thesis, 1998), p. 3. Four gallons is a conservative estimate; other scientists estimate up to seven gallons a minute. The 3rd edition of Bigelow and Schroeder's authoritative *Fishes of the Gulf of Maine*, ed. Bruce B. Collette and Grace Klein-MacPhee (Washington: Smithsonian Institution Press, 2002) gives four to seven gallons (15-28 liters) per minute (p. 135).

5. Sara Gottlieb, interview, August 28, 2000.

6. In 1955, the estimated population of adult Atlantic menhaden (that is, age three and over) was 1.591 billion; by 1999 it was 204.7 million. The annual catch had plummeted from a peak of 712 thousand metric tons in 1956 to 171.2 million tons in 1999. These figures come from the Atlantic Menhaden Management Review, 2000 (Tables 1 and 2), a report to the Atlantic States Marine Fisheries Commission prepared by the Atlantic Menhaden Advisory Committee, a group dominated by representatives of the menhaden reduction industry.

7. Roger Williams, A Key to the Language of America (London, 1643), p. 114; Goode, pp. 10-11; "Menhaden," *The American Heritage Dictionary of the English Language:* Fourth Edition (Boston: Houghton Mifflin, 2000).

8. Much of this analysis is drawn from William Cronon, *Changes in the Land: Indians, Colonists, and the Ecology of New England* (New York: Hill & Wang,

1983), pp. 149-151. The only error in Cronon's fine discussion comes from ignoring the role of fish fertilizer in Indian agriculture.

9. George Brown Goode, *The Fisheries and Fishery Industries of the United States*, Section V, Volume I (Washington 1887), pp. 367, 371-372; in this report prepared for the U.S. Commission of Fish and Fisheries, Goode includes almost forty folio pages in fine print from a fascinating 300-page manuscript diary of a farmer-fisherman who traces the evolution of these companies. Ralph H. Gabriel, "Geographic Influences in the Development of the Menhaden Fishery on the Eastern Coast of the United States," *The Geographical Review*, Vol. 10, No. 2 (August 1920), 91-100, p. 94; Ralph Henry Gabriel, *The Evolution of Long Island* (New Haven: Yale University Press, 1921; Reprint edition, Port Washington, Long Island: Ira J. Friedman, 1968), p. 79.

10. Gabriel, 1920, p. 94.

11. Lance E. Davis, Robert E. Gallman, and Karin Gleiter, *In Pursuit of Leviathan: Technology, Institutions, Productivity, and Profits in American Whaling, 1816-1906* (Chicago: University of Chicago Press, 1997), pp. 19, 28, 30. Baleen was widely known as "whalebone." Although this book correctly distinguishes between the oil derived from sperm whales ("sperm oil") and that from all other whales ("whale oil"), for simplicity I lump the two together under the latter term.

12. Goode, 1887, p. 361; also Goode, 1880, p. 190.

13. Goode, 1887, p. 360; Barbara J. Garrity-Blake, *The Fish Factory: Work and Meaning for Black and White Fishermen of the Menhaden Industry* (Knoxville: University of Tennessee Press, 1994), p. 18.

14. Goode, 1887, p. 334; Davis, p. 19.

15. Herman Melville, *Moby-Dick; Or, The Whale* (Evanston and Chicago: Northwestern University Press and the Newberry Library, 1988), Chapter 6.

16. "A New Enterprise," *New Bedford Standard*, reprinted in *Scientific American*, Vol. 9, No. 6, August 8, 1863, p. 96.

17. "Chasing the Bony-Fish," *New York Times*, May 26, 1884, p. 5.

18. John Frye, *The Men All Singing: The Story of Menhaden Fishing,* 2nd edition (n.p.: The Donning Company, 1999), pp. 50, 52, 54, 76. Frye has some marvelous details about the spectacular growth of Reedville as well as pages of pictures of these mansions. In 1984, Reedville's historic district was placed on the Virginia Landmarks Register.

19. Goode, 1880, pp. 162-163; "The Menhaden Oil Mania," *Scientific American,* Vol. 16, No. 10, March 9, 1867, p. 154.

20. Davis, p. 41.

21. "The Way Menhaden Oil Is Made," *Scientific American,* Vol. 7, No. 13, September 27, 1862, p. 198; "The Newport Fisheries," *Scientific American,* Vol. 10, No. 12, March 19, 1864, p. 178. These articles from *Scientific American* were first discussed by Nathan Adams in two unpublished 2005 papers: "'Not Without Value': Menhaden, Fertilizer, Oil & a Migratory Fishery in the 19th and Early 20th Century" and "Closing Destiny: The Menhaden Fishery of the 19th and Early 20th Century."

22. "Menhaden Oil Mania," p. 154.

23. "Eastern Long Island—Menhaden Oil and the Fisheries," *Scientific American,* Vol. 25, No. 2, January 7, 1871, p. 21.

24. Gilbert Burling, "Long Island Oil-Fisheries," *Appleton's Journal of Literature, Science and Art,* Vol. 6, No. 127, September 2, 1871, pp. 268-273.

25. "Menhaden Oil Mania," p. 154.

26. Davis, p. 15.

27. Sperm whales sometimes contained the precious but rare ambergris used in some pricey perfumes, and the sailors themselves often did use whale teeth as canvases for their etched art known as scrimshaw. Also, what was left of the blubber after the oil was tried out was used to feed the flames of the try works.

28. "Manure from the Sea (from *The Maine Farmer*)," *Southern Planter,* June 1855, p. 169.

29. "Artificial Guano from Fish," *The Cultivator,* June 1856, p. 17. See also, "Manufacture of Fish Guano," *New England Farmer,* July 1856, p. 335, and "Menhaden Oil," Plough, the Loom and the Anvil, October 1857, p. 213.

30. Goode, 1880, pp. 90-91.

31. Rob Leon Greer, The Menhaden Industry of the Atlantic Coast: Appendix III to the *Report of the U.S. Commissioner of Fisheries for 1914* (Washington: GPO, 1915), p. 5. Greer incorrectly states that the Ranger was the first floating menhaden factory; at least two and possibly four were already operating in Long Island Sound. Frye, p. 50, gives a few more details about the Ranger.

32. Report by Edward J. Boyd in *Rural New-Yorker* reprinted in *Scientific American,* Vol. 41, No. 22, November 29, 1879, p. 344.

33. Charles Burr Todd, "The Menhaden Fishery and Factories," *Lippincott's Magazine of Popular Literature and Science,* December 1883, 545-556, p. 546.

34. Ibid, pp. 546, 555.

35. "Food Fishes of America: How They Are Caught on Our Coasts, Lakes, and Rivers," *New York Times,* May 30, 1874, p. 10.

36. Goode, 1880, pp. 114, 164-165, 185.

37. "Menhaden Season Closed," *New York Times,* December 16, 1888, p. 14.

38. Thomas Henry Huxley, "Inaugural Address," The Fisheries Exhibition, London, 1883.C

39. "The Menhaden Question," *Forest and Stream,* Vol. 28, No. 6, March 3, 1887, p. 111.

40. See "Threaten to Fire Upon Jersey Fishing Pirates," *New York Times,* September 29, 1922.

41. See Cronon, Changes in the Land, pp. 132-134, on this ongoing effort to wipe out wolves to protect livestock.

42. Among freshwater fish or saltwater shellfish, we have long relished scavengers such as catfish and crabs, or filter feeders, such as oysters, mussels, and clams. Then there is the recent introduction of that farm-raised herbivore originally from the Nile delta, the tilapia, for anyone who doesn't mind eating completely tasteless flesh.

43. "Questions of Food Fish," *New York Times*, September 10, 1882, p. 8.

44. Leonard C. Roy, "Menhaden—Uncle Sam's Top Commercial Fish," *National Geographic*, June 1949, 813-823, p. 813.

45. "Biggest Ocean Harvest: The lowly menhaden, top U.S. commercial fish, is hunted by scientifically equipped task force," *LIFE*, November 19, 1951, pp. 140-142

46. Frye, p. 52.

McNeal Edwards machine shop

Eastern Long Island

Shelter Island —

Jessup's Neck —

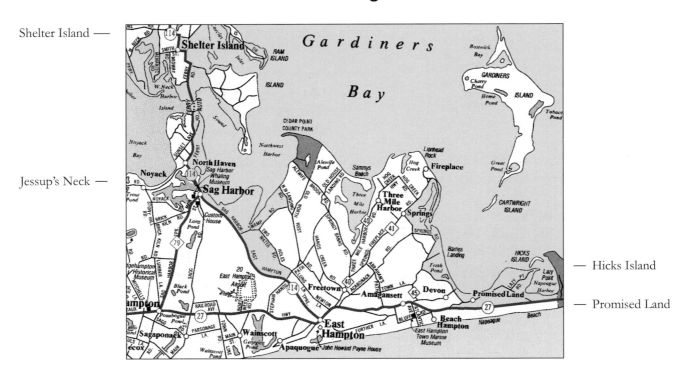

— Hicks Island

— Promised Land

New York City is to the left (west), and Montauk to the right (east)

Chapter 2: The Early Days of Menhaden Fishing on Long Island

by William Wise*

Long Island's farmer/fishermen began regularly seining local waters for menhaden in the years after the American Revolution. The fish were used as farm fertilizer, either whole or ground up and combined with other organic materials, such as manure, swamp dirt and human "night soil." When fish were brought to the beach, they were loaded into wagons or carts and moved to the fields. By the 1840s, numerous fishing "gangs" had organized and staked their claim to specific beaches of Long Island's coastline, especially in the Peconic Bay system and Great South Bay. This shore seining was a seasonal activity, done mainly in late spring and early fall. The other major use of menhaden before the Civil War was as bait in the offshore line fisheries for cod, haddock and mackerel.

---

*Associate Director of SUNY Stony Brook's School of Marine and Atmospheric Sciences and Director of the School's Living Marine Resources Institute (LMRI).

The Industrial Revolution in North America created an increasing demand for oil to be used in a wide variety of manufacturing processes starting early in the 19th century. The earliest attempts to wring oil from menhaden were made in Rhode Island in the 1820s, but the industry did not burgeon until mid-century. Then, the Civil War raised demand for oil to new heights and the whaling industry began to decline as whale stocks became depleted. This propelled the search for alternative sources of oil and the menhaden reduction fishery expanded rapidly in the years after 1860. Menhaden oil found a wide variety of industrial uses: as a component of oleomargarine; tanning animal hides; in the manufacture of soap and use as illuminating and lubricating oil.

The menhaden reduction industry began in 1847, when "Judge" Marcus Osborn set up a basic pot works on or near Jessup's Neck in the hamlet of Noyac, in the Town of Southampton. The Osborn family had purchased Jessup's Neck and a parcel of the adjacent mainland from the Jessup family in 1800. The Osborn farm was a large, progressive and prosperous one during

"Haul-seine fishing on Long Island, 1790 to 1850; taking out the fish" (original caption, from Goode)

Purse-seine fishing (from Wikipedia)

The old haul seine (above) was less efficient than the purse seine invented in the 1860s. The new purse seine (left) could completely enclose a school of menhaden. Its top floats keep one edge on the surface of the water. Weights placed on the bottom keep the other edge below the school of fish. When the lines at the net's bottom edge are tightened through rings, they close the net like a draw-string purse and a large school of fish can be caught. (RF)]

the 19th century. The beach along both sides of the long, thin neck was good seining ground and menhaden were regularly caught and applied whole to the fields as fertilizer, the excess fish being pressed for their oil. Jessup's Neck is now part of the Elizabeth A. Morton National Wildlife Refuge administered by the U.S. Fish and Wildlife Service.

The pot works established on Jessup's Neck was likely a primitive affair. Such facilities at the time were little more than iron try pots of the type used in the whaling industry placed atop an open wood fire in which whole menhaden were boiled. The separation of oil from fish flesh was made more complete through the progressive application of mechanical pressure in the form of a descending lid of some sort. As the oil was expressed, it rose to the surface and, upon cooling, was decanted off into barrels. The fish flesh remaining after the oil was extracted was subsequently dried, pulverized and otherwise processed into fish "scrap" to be sold and used as fertilizer (and, beginning in the 1920's, as a component in prepared animal foods).

Pot Works Appear on Long Island's Coast

Word spread of the success of the Jessup's Neck works, and of others then being established in Connecticut, Rhode Island and Maine at roughly the same time. Pot works began to appear in many areas of Long Island's coast, especially along the shores of the Peconic and Gardiners Bays. In the face of rising demand and high oil prices, the technology for extracting oil from fish rapidly grew more sophisticated and the size and capacity of the reduction facilities increased. Many "pot works" grew into "fish factories." An important advance was the substitution of steam heat for wood fires as the heat source in reduction plants. Because steam heat is more efficient, the temperature in the cooking vats was more easily controlled. On July 4, 1850, Daniel D. Wells of Greenport and his eldest son, H. E. Wells, opened New York's first steam-powered menhaden reduction facility, at Chequit Point on Shelter Island (*'chequit'* is a local Native American word for weakfish).

Shelter Island

Shelter Island in the 1850's and 1860's was not the summer resort community that it later became. The Island's population was comprised largely of farmers, fishermen and small merchants. The Island's waters for many years were teeming with menhaden from May through October, and Shelter Island became the locus of New York's nascent menhaden industry. By 1866, 18 fish factories lined the Island's coast. Additional plants were found along isolated stretches of the Peconic Bay shoreline, the Great South Bay, and on Jamaica Bay's Barren Island. Through the 1860s, 1870s and into the 1880s, New York was at the epicenter of a burgeoning industry that stretched from Maine to Virginia.

All photographs in this chapter were taken on Hicks Island in Napeague Bay.

Napeague

Menhaden reduction plants were first established on Napeague (na-PEE-gue) Harbor in the late 1850s and early 1860s, as the Trustees of the Town of East Hampton began to issue a series of leases to individuals for what they termed "oil stations" or "fishing stations" on the harbor's eastern shore. The likely attraction of the east shore of Napeague Harbor was the tongue of relatively deep water that hugs that shoreline for most of its length, providing good vessel access to the piers and docks of these facilities. Eventually, three plants were constructed on Napeague Harbor. Records suggest that the ownership of each facility changed hands several times during the 1860s and 1870s. The latest mention recorded of a menhaden plant on Napeague Harbor was in 1884, when the plant owned by William Tuthill & Sons apparently closed.

Fish factory in Napeague (from Goode)

Promised Land

In the early 1870s, Shelter Island's increasing popularity as a site for religiously-affiliated camps and wealthy summer visitors began to put pressure on the owners of the odiferous fish factories to close or relocate off the island. By 1880, only two factories remained in operation on the Island. By then, the locus of New York's menhaden industry had shifted to a nearby but hitherto barren stretch of Long Island coastline—Promised Land.

Promised Land is located along the north side of the Napeague isthmus fronting on Napeague Bay, about three miles east of Amagansett, in the Town of East Hampton. The first menhaden factory established at Promised Land was apparently built by Captain B.C. Cartwright, who relocated his facility from Shelter Island to the new site in 1872. Several additional plants were built in the late 1870s. By 1880, six factories were in operation at Promised Land.

Promised Land plants, arranged from west-to east

• Ragged Edge Oil Works, owned by Ellsworth Tuthill & Co. and built in 1879. This large plant was one of three at Promised Land that was still in business in the late 1890s, when much of the East Coast menhaden industry was consolidated under a single corporate owner (see below)

• Jonas Smith & Company, which was founded in 1876 and remained in business through the late 1880s.

• Ranger Oil Company, owned by T.F. Price & Company. Price who had, as other owners, purchased a derelict steamer in 1866 and converted it into a floating menhaden factory. In the early 1870s, he berthed the "Ranger" on a semi-permanent basis at Promised Land. In 1879, he purchased the adjacent shore land at Promised Land from Captain Joshua Edwards and built a factory on it. Ranger Oil Company survived until the late 1890's, when it was bought up by an East Coast menhaden syndicate.

• Novelty Oil and Guano Works, owned by Hiram Dixon. This was originally constructed as a "phosphate works" at Promised Land, buying fish scrap from the menhaden plants and combining it with other materials to produce fertilizer. As the menhaden plants began to sell their own scrap as fertilizer, this supply dried up for Dixon. In 1879, he converted his phosphate works to a menhaden reduction plant. The plant was in operation from 1879 to 1888, when it was bought and dismantled by the owner of the adjacent Falcon Oil Works, George F. Tuthill.

• Falcon Oil Works, owned by George F. Tuthill and built in 1879. Among the larger factories at Promised Land, this facility was still in operation in the late 1890s when purchased by the East Coast menhaden syndicate.

• Montauk Oil Works, owned by W. A. Abbe & Co. Little information is available on this factory, which was constructed around 1880 and put up for sale in 1889.

Why was Promised Land chosen as a new site for this industrial concentration, rather than expanding the number of plants on Napeague Harbor? The reason is not clear, but several factors may have contributed. Along the east side of Napeague Harbor, relatively deep water runs close to the beach in front of Promised Land. There is more linear shoreline length at Promised Land than on the east side of Napeague Harbor. Finally, and most important, the mouth of Napeague Harbor between Goff Point and the east side of Hicks Island is subject to severe shoaling. This channel was extremely narrow in the late 19th century and the currents very strong, constantly shifting sand in the area. If the channel was thus at times unnavigable, the factories within the Harbor would have been isolated. Located on the open coast of Napeague Bay, vessel access to a factory at Promised Land would not be subject to the vagaries of a capricious inlet.

With the proliferation of the fish factories during the 1870s, an entire seasonal community developed at Promised Land to support the increasing pace of economic activity. Dormitories were built for African-Americans who, beginning in the late 1870s, were brought up from Virginia, Georgia and other southern states to work at the reduction plants during the fishing season. Various ships chandlery, food and general supplies stores catered to the needs of the steamers and their crews that delivered the fish to the factories, as well as to the factory workers.

How did Promised Land get its name? Various explanations have been proposed. One explanation is that it was so named by a mail carrier who periodically undertook the long and arduous trip from East Hampton to Promised Land. After traversing the desolate wastes of the western portion of the Napeague isthmus, when the brick chimneys of the fish factories finally hove into sight, he felt he had reached the "promised land." Another story attributes the name to African-Americans who worked in the factories during the season. The steady and gainful employment that the factories offered each summer made the area a "promised land" of sorts. Lastly, some accounts suggest that the site was named by George F. Tuthill, owner of one of the larger factories at Promised Land. What might have been in

Mr. Tuthill's mind? Perhaps the significant wealth that he and some of the other factory owners expected to (and did) extract from their works there. Alternatively, given the exodus of menhaden plants from Shelter Island in the early 1870s as that island gentrified, the lonesome, sandy wastes along the north side of Napeague might truly have seemed a promised land to Mr. Tuthill and his fellow plant owners.

Hicks Island

Just east of Promised Land lies Hicks Island, an isolated strip of sand that, over long periods of time, is periodically connected with the Napeague isthmus, depending on the continual drift of sand moving along this exposed shoreline. A menhaden factory on Hicks Island was first constructed in 1879 by William P. Green, the son of M. P. Green, owner of one of the Napeague Harbor plants. The second owner of the Hicks Island facility was O. H. Bishop, who operated it as the Excelsior Oil Works. (The photographs in this chapter derive from the Hicks Island ruins).

The Salad Years

Through the 1860s and 1870s, New York dominated the East Coast menhaden fishery, which then encompassed the area between Maine and Virginia. By 1875 coal-powered steamers were replacing sailing sloops and "yachts" in the fishery. This quickened the trip to and from the fishing grounds, and the steamers, less susceptible to the set of the wind, allowed for more regular and predictable arrival times at the plant. As the size and capacity of the plants grew, there was a trend towards greater vertical integration in the menhaden fishery. Independent boat owners were bought out by plant owners, who henceforth controlled the fishing as well as the processing sectors of the menhaden industry. In 1877, 23 factories were in operation around Long Island's coast, 15 on the East End and 8 along the shores of the Great South Bay and Jamaica Bay's Barren Island. In contrast, factories in other states in the same year numbered only 36 altogether. The steamers at Promised Land fished throughout Long Island Sound, Block Island Sound and in the near-shore waters of the Atlantic Ocean from Montauk down to the New Jersey shore. Fish were to be found further afield from Long Island along the coast, but the long delivery times to the Promised Land factories from these distant areas risked significant spoilage of the catch and spoiled fish did not process well.

With the exception of an isolated poor fishing year, catches delivered to the factories at Promised Land and Hicks Island remained high through the mid-1880s. However, 1887 saw a dramatic decline in the abundance of menhaden. In addition, oil and guano prices were depressed because of increased U.S. imports of cheaper tanning oils from France and England and fertilizers from South America, excessive U.S. production in previous years and cutthroat competition among U.S. plant owners. Several Promised Land factories remained idle that year.

Cooperation, then Consolidation

In the face of a more limited supply of fish and competition from overseas producers, menhaden factory owners in New York and elsewhere along the East Coast, in the interest of their own economic survival, began to cooperate with one another. They agreed, for example, to the start and end dates of the annual fishing season. However, continued low availability of menhaden from 1890 to 1894, especially from Long Island north, brought about a significant consolidation of the industry, with some of the smaller plants closing and/or being bought out by larger operators. The relatively small factories on Great South Bay did not survive this period. At Promised Land, W. A. Abbe & Co.'s Montauk Oil Works closed in 1889. Hiram Dixon's factory was purchased by Rhode Island's D. F. Church in 1881, who sold it to his next-door neighbor, G. F. Tuthill, in 1888. On Hicks Island, Excelsior Oil Works' assets were seized in 1893 for failure to make mortgage payments and these assets were sold in 1894. Between 1894 and 1910, the site on Hicks Island lay derelict.

By 1896, only the three largest of the original plants remained at Promised Land: Falcon Oil Works, Ranger Oil Works and Ellsworth Tuthill & Co. Other New York factories still operating that year were on Shelter Island (Hawkins Brothers), Raynor's factory at Cedar Point near the entrance to Northwest Harbor and a plant on Jamaica Bay's Barren Island.

In the spring of 1890, representatives of an English syndicate had arrived in the United States to conduct a survey of the menhaden reduction industry on the eastern end of Long Island. The syndicate had developed a fish rendering and processing system that required far fewer hands to operate and delivered greater production and cost efficiencies than were offered by the technologies used in the menhaden fishery of the time. In the fall of 1897, the syndicate announced its intention to purchase the assets of the independent owners of the twenty factories, the steamers and related equipment, which constituted the menhaden reduction industry north of Chesapeake Bay. The syndicate representatives met with the owners of the factories and offered to purchase their collective assets or, in time, drive them out of business once they got a toe-hold in the menhaden fishery. An industry leader, Nathaniel B. Church, who had visited England to inspect the new processing technology, convinced the American companies that they could not compete with a factory employing the new process. The owners of seventeen of the plants from Delaware north along the East Coast agreed to sell, including the owners of all the plants in New York. The aggregate price was $1 million.

The American Fisheries Company (AFC) was incorporated in New Jersey in 1898, with Nathaniel B. Church as vice-president and manager. Many of the previous owners of the reduction plants bought stock in the new company. AFC employed the same fleet of steamers, their captains and crew that fished for the independent owners. The company operated factories in the following locations: four small factories at Booth Bay and Round Pond, Maine; one large factory at Tiverton, Rhode Island; three factories at Promised Land and three factories at Lewes, Delaware. Of the eight factories purchased in New York, five were dismantled and their equipment relocated to the three factories at

Promised Land or another of the company's plants. The corporate headquarters of the company was located in Greenport, Long Island. AFC steamers were over-wintered at Greenport or Tiverton, Rhode Island, where the company maintained full-service shipyards.

After 1898, New York's menhaden reduction industry was located solely at Promised Land. Of the three factories at Promised Land previously owned by Ellsworth Tuthill, one was converted into a fertilizer plant and leased back to its previous owner. The Falcon Oil Company, previously owned by G. F. Tuthill, and the Ranger Oil Company, previously owned by T. F. Price, were remodeled with new boilers and steam cookers, a fish elevator and fish bin. For the first time, the factories were equipped with electric lights. A branch track of the Long Island Railroad was laid to Promised Land to facilitate the shipment of products from the plants.

In general, 1899 saw poor catches of menhaden from the waters regularly fished by the boats out of Promised Land. Things got worse on September 17, 1899, when the ex-Falcon Oil Company factory burned down, leaving the ex-Ranger Oil Company and the fertilizer plant as the only facilities still operating at Promised Land.

The years 1900 and 1901 had good seasons at Promised Land, with large catches and significant additions made to the plant's processing capacity, but the financial condition of AFC was poor. In early 1900, the firm went into receivership. The assets of the company were transferred to a paper firm, the US Menhaden Oil & Guano Co., and then assigned to a new firm, The Fisheries Company (TFC), incorporated in New Jersey and the successor to AFC.

In 1902, the newly-designed American Process screw press was given a trial at Promised Land. Previous menhaden-processing technology involved dumping steamed fish into wheeled cars with slatted sides. The cars were moved beneath vertical hydraulic presses, the press descended with force, squeezing the oil and water from the steamed fish out through the spaces between the slats. This left behind the solid material, which was

American Process Screw Press. 1901 Photograph

eventually dumped from the car and processed as fish scrap. The new screw press was essentially a horizontal cone with openings at both ends. Its sides were slatted and through its center ran a central shaft shaped like a screw. As the shaft rotated, boiled fish fed into a large hopper at the front of the device were gradually transported towards the other end. Since the diameter of the cone decreased along its length, the material came under ever greater pressure as it moved along the length of the press, forcing the oil and water through the slats on the side. Eventually, the scrap remaining was forced out of the opening at the narrow end of the cone. The screw press had several advantages over the vertical hydraulic press: it could run continuously, the fish to be processed

75

did not need to be "batched," and the press could be fed by a conveyor belt at the front end and emptied of pressed scrap by a conveyor belt at the opposite end, requiring little, if any human labor.

The new screw press was considered a success. Over the winter of 1902/1903, the plant at Promised Land was torn down and a new plant constructed. Eight screw presses were installed on the second floor, so that the oil and water pressed from the fish would flow by gravity to the tanks in the oil room on the ground floor. Previously, presses were typically located on the ground floor and the expelled liquids had to be pumped to the oil room. Other equipment was added to the plant to make the reduction process as automated as possible. In 1903, TFC's factory at Tiverton, Rhode Island was dismantled and relocated to Promised Land.

During the years 1900 to 1905 catches of menhaden were excellent, and the facilities at Promised Land were kept busy. In 1905, TFC purchased the assets of its largest rival in the menhaden fishery, The Atlantic

Fisheries Company, based in Virginia. Catches remained high in 1906, and at the end of the year TFC was purchased by the Wharton Fisheries Company, owned by the industrialist Joseph Wharton (see Chapter 3).

The Gradual Decline of the Menhaden Fishing Industry: 1907 until 1970

The Promised Land facilities continued to operate un-der the TFC name. Menhaden catches dropped off sig-nificantly in 1907: fish delivered to the Promised Land plants were in poor condition and produced a low yield of oil. Partly in response to these conditions, some of the fishing steamers were outfitted with cold stor-age units to better preserve the quality of the delivered fish. On July 31, 1907, the main Promised Land fac-tory burned to the ground due to a fire that apparently began in the automatic scrap dryer. The water pumps available to fight the fire were in the dryer room and thus inaccessible to those attempting to put the fire out. Except for the docks, the plant was a complete loss. The poor catches and the catastrophic fire dealt a death blow to TFC and, on October 20, 1907, the company went into receivership. Soon thereafter, remnants of the factory were removed from the site. The fertilizer plant on the west end of Promised Land had been torn down several years earlier. Thus, during 1908, there were no

operations related to the menhaden fishery conducted at or out of Promised Land.

In 1909, the New York City based fertilizer and import firm Heller, Hirsch and Company began to construct a new factory at Promised Land. The corporate entity operating the plant was the Atlantic Fertilizer and Oil Company (AFOC). By the start of that year's fishing season, the factory was not fully equipped to handle the volume of fish available and little oil was produced. In mid-summer of that year, G. F. Tuthill, previously of the Falcon Oil Company, began construction of the Triton Fertilizer and Oil Company factory at Promised Land, which went into operation in 1910.

In 1910, Hicks Island was resurrected when its exist-ing derelict plant was purchased and refurbished by the Neptune Fishing Company, a subsidiary of the Consoli-dated Fisheries Company. In the same year, C. A. Sick-ler Brothers of Wilkes-Barre, Pennsylvania, purchased AFOC and its plants at Promised Land and Round Pond, Maine, although these facilities continued to op-

erate under the AFOC name. Thus, during 1910 three plants were in operation at or near Promised Land: the AFOC and Triton plants at Promised Land, and the Neptune Fishing Company plant on Hicks Island.

The year 1911 had a very good season at Promised Land and throughout the menhaden fishery. By season's end, AFOC had acquired the factory on Hicks Island, although it continued to operate under the Neptune Fishing Company. However, by the end of the 1912 fishing season, AFOC was having difficulty making payroll on its steamers and at its Promised Land plant. In 1913, the Atlantic Phosphate and Oil Corporation was established through the merger of AFOC, Neptune Fishing Company and The Menhaden Fishing Company (Lewes, Delaware) The latter firm owned and operated steamers only.

Although the Atlantic Phosphate and Oil Corporation continued to improve its Promised Land and Hicks Island factories, by the end of 1914 that company, too, failed and went into receivership. The 19 steamers and the factory at Promised Land were purchased by Seaboard Fisheries Company in 1915. The Hicks Island plant was bought by Swan and Finch Company, a subsidiary of the Standard Oil Company.

In 1915 and 1916, three plants were in operation: the Triton and Seaboard Fisheries plants at Promised Land, and the Swan and Finch plant on Hicks Island.

The menhaden fishery at Promised Land and all along the East Coast slumped during 1917 and 1918 as many of the steamers were requisitioned by the U.S. government, or sold to the British and Canadian governments, to serve as minesweepers and other auxiliary craft during World War I. After the war, these ships were returned to their original owners and resumed menhaden fishing.

In 1917, the Consolidated Fisheries Company reacquired the Hicks Island factory. Of the two plants at Promised Land, only the Triton factory was operational in 1917 and 1918; the Seacoast Fisheries plant was closed.

In June 1919, The Consolidated Fisheries Company bought the inactive Seacoast Fisheries factory at Promised Land and suspended operations at its smaller Hicks Island facility. The Hicks Island factory was subsequently dismantled and never rebuilt. Menhaden fishing was good from 1919-1923 and the Consolidated Fisheries and Triton factories at Promised Land were busy, but in 1924 the Consolidated Fisheries Company filed for bankruptcy because of very poor catches that year. Its Promised Land plant continued to operate through mid-1929, when it was closed for good for lack of fish. The Triton plant had an active year in 1925 but catches began to drop off the following year. In 1931, the Triton plant burned down and all menhaden activity at Promised Land ceased.

Promised Land lay derelict until 1933, when the Smith Meal Company purchased and began to renovate the re

maining factory and associated docks. The Smith Meal plant continued in operation until 1969. In the early 1960s, the abundance of menhaden declined dramatically, especially in waters north of New Jersey. Beginning in 1963, the Promised Land plant began to take in and rend large amounts of so-called "trash fish." This included skates, sea robins, red hake, and others, which were often caught in the trawl fisheries but there was little demand and prices were low for these fish. For a few years, very large catches of trash species kept the plant active, but this fishery was not sustainable. In 1969, the Promised Land plant closed for good and much of its equipment was shipped to the company's factory in Port Monmouth, New Jersey. This ended the history of the menhaden reduction fishery in New York, although for a number of subsequent years, menhaden steamers fishing for reduction plants located in New Jersey and Rhode Island made significant catches in New York State waters, especially in Long Island Sound.

All color photographs were taken from
a fishing boat circling Crab Island.

Chapter 3: Fish Factory Ruins on Crab Island, New Jersey

by Ruth Formanek

The ruins of a fish factory stand on 100 desolate acres on Crab Island, near Tuckerton, and northwest of Atlantic City, in New Jersey. The burned-out and decayed structures are known locally as "The Stinkhouse" and for obvious reasons, as fish processing was a smelly enterprise.

The fish processed at the factory were menhaden or 'bunkers.' Laws governed their catching from May to October: not less than 90 feet from Sandy Hook Bay, Raritan Bay and Delaware Bay, not closer than 6/10 of a nautical mile from shore. No fishing was allowed on Saturday, Sunday, Memorial Day, Labor Day, or Fourth of July, according to Lori Edmunds (2008).[1] New Jersey was one of many Atlantic coast states which regulated the catching of menhaden.

The history of the Crab Island factory is sketchy. Buildings are first mentioned in 1846, a factory, in a 1902 deed, purchased by the Newport Fertilizer company for $6500, as 'Fish Oil Works.' According to newspaper clippings collected by the Tuckerton, NJ, Historical Society, the factory changed owners every few years, as did the factories on Long Island (see Chapter 2) and those in Reedville, VA (see Chapter 1), their fortunes varying with the size of the menhaden catch.

According to newspaper clippings from the 1880s: "Francis French [from Tuckerton] now owns and will run the menhaden oil factory, formerly owned and managed by Capt. C.N. Smith. Mr. Smith has gone into the cultivation of small fruits at Lower Bank, quite extensively, putting out thousands of strawberries of late and fine varieties."[2]

Mr. William A. Sooy, the manager of Mr. Wharton's interests in this part of the state, reported that, though fish are 'scarce or shy,' over 600,000 were caught up to last week. The fish caught now are yielding six gallons of oil per thousand, a good yield.[3]

The second clipping above refers to "Joseph Wharton, Quaker, Industrial Pioneer" (Yates, 1987)[4] who eventually created a menhaden-processing monopoly in the area. He was born in Philadelphia, PA, in 1826 to Quaker parents. After ventures in several branches of business, Wharton began to buy stock in a zinc operation near Bethlehem, PA, then in nickel ore, forming the American Nickel Works, and later the Bethlehem Steel Company. In the 1880's Wharton bought large tracts of southern New Jersey as well as a menhaden-processing factory which produced oil and fertilizer on Crab Island, and three steamers. He enlarged his business by buying a fish fertilizer plant in Milford, Connecticut.

Toward the beginning of the Spanish-American War the menhaden industry consolidated and formed a syndicate. Always buying and selling, Wharton offered to sell the syndicate his various interests but the syndicate was unresponsive. He then offered one of his steamers to the federal government but without success. Wharton put his fishing properties into the Newport Fertilizer Company which became the Wharton Fisheries Company. He acquired control over the Cape Fear Fisheries Company of South Carolina and, in 1906, he purchased the syndicate. The combination of the three companies was capitalized at three million dollars; its properties included 41 steamships and eight plants for making fish oil and fertilizer, and employed about 2,600 people.

These transactions gave Wharton a monopoly over the menhaden industry of the Atlantic coast. He remained active in philanthropy, international commerce and politics until his death in 1909. Today he is known for founding the Wharton School of Business at the University of Pennsylvania and for helping to create Swarthmore College.

The ships of the menhaden fleet were made of wood until 1948, when steel, and later aluminum, replaced wood. About 125 to 200 ft in length, each boat had two purse boats, about 25 feet long. When a school of menhaden was located by a spotter in the crows nest of the large boat, the smaller boats would surround the school with a huge net, weighted at the bottom with lead and kept buoyant by large corks attached to the top. These purse seine nets were about 90 feet wide and 900 feet long. When the drawstring at the bottom of the purse was closed, the fish were trapped in the net. The big boat pulled in the net and huge pumps delivered the fish to the factory.

After World War II, fish-processing plants added piper cubs to search for schools of menhaden. The pilots would look for seagulls active on the water, or for large oil slicks caused by the oily fish. When the fish were spotted, their location was radioed to the captain of the boat. After they were filled to capacity, the boats would return to the factory. Before their arrival at the island, a siren alerted the ground crew to be ready for unloading. Crews had to be prepared to process the catch imme-diately to keep it from spoiling. (Apparently processing was not always swift in view of the factory's name—the Stinkhouse). The fish were then put on a conveyor belt to go through a counter, and a bell would ring for each thousand fish caught. In 1953, scales replaced the counters, and from then on 746 pounds equalled 1,000 fish. The fish were put into a big storage bin to await processing.

The boat's crew, around 18 men, lived on board; they were paid by the number of fish they caught, the captain receiving 52 cents per 1,000 fish, and the crew 18 to 26 cents depending on their job. The best season was 1958, when the total catch from late May to October was 210 million. The factory employed mostly southern African-Americans, who worked in 12 hour shifts. They lived on the island in bunkhouses provided by the company and left New Jersey after the season was over, in November.

John Frye (1978)[4] describes the heavy labor demanded pulling in the heavy seines filled with menhaden. "If the captain knew he had an extra large set—half a mil-

George W. Mills factory in Milford, Connecticut, in 1877, later bought by Joseph Wharton.

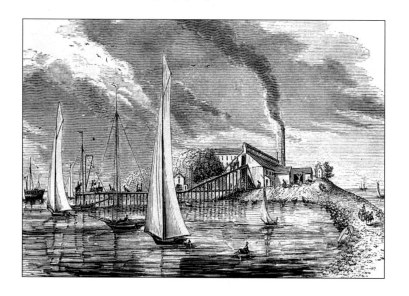

The Barnegat and the West Beaufort

The Crab Island factory owned six boats of the Menhaden Fleet: the Barnegat, the Beach Haven, the Seagerth, the Texas, the Manasquan, and the Palm Beach.

lion or more fish—that could not be raised by his own men, he might sound four blasts on a whistle or horn for a sister ship to help…At first the net came up yard by yard. The men's fingers clawed into the mesh. Their shoulder and back muscles flexed. With a heavy set it soon came to a point where muscle was not enough. Then the captain called out, 'Charles, start up a chantey!' The verses came out of the chanteyman's store of couplets built up over his years of fishing. A good chanteyman was a prize. With light sets [of fish] there was no singing. But when that heavy set came, when the purse boats had surrounded 200,000 or more fish, and all knew there was work ahead to get them into the hold before they died to become dead weight, inspiration came to the chanteyman."

Frye quotes several chanteys that seem to be part of the southern work song tradition with its gospel roots. Many of the chanteys have been saved in the collections of the Library of Congress.

"Chanteyman: All the weight's on the mate's boat!
Fishermen: Hey, hey, honey!

Chanteyman: We gonna save them if we can!
Fishermen: Hey, hey, honey!
Chanteyman: She's long and she's tall!
Fishermen: Hey, hey, honey! Long and tall!
Chanteyman: Want to see her—!
Fishermen: Hey, hey, honey!
Chanteyman: I have a girl in Baltimore! Hey, hey, honey!
Fishermen: Streetcar runs right by her door! Hey, hey, honey!"

Most of the chanting was heard only by the fishermen but, according to Frye, who quotes observers, "Sometimes yachts came out for the performances. Some even tied up to the purse boats, just to hear the men singing. It sounded like a band out there on the water."

In contrast to the fishermen and workers, the managers of the plant were mostly from town. They worked through the winter in eight-hour shifts, doing maintenance work, and had their own dining room, separate from the workmen.

Processing began with the menhaden going from the storage box to the cookers. There were six cookers, about 30 feet long and 36 inches in diameter. Inside, there was a continuous conveyor screw, and steam jets would cook the fish. The fish next went to the six pressers which pressed out water, oil and blood. The liquid would drip on a grated floor, flow into a gutter and was pumped to one of the ten separators. The separators worked on centrifugal force to separate oil, which could be used, from other liquids. Oil was lighter and would stay on the inside of the machine, from where it was pumped to storage tanks. The squeezed fish were put on a conveyer to one of the six driers. The dried fish scrap was stored in a shed. As needed, scrap was put on a conveyer to the grinding mill and made into a fine meal.

The plant was also used for a few years by Atlantic City to burn garbage until 1930. In the early 1940s the original buildings were torn down and new ones built. Edmunds states that the Smith family maintained ownership of the property beginning in 1940 with the Fish Products Company, then the Smith Meal Company from 1972 to 1973. The Smith Meal Company also owned a fish factory in Napeague, Long Island, NY. Title was transferred to American Farm Products, Inc., then Hanson Properties, Inc., from April 1974 to August 1974. From 1965 to 1969, as the factory no longer caught its own fish, processed fish scrap was shipped to Crab Island by railroad and boat from Louisiana.

Crab Island was a big operation. It had its own general store which offered everything from candy to clothes. In 1947 the company put up a water tower. Once active with as many as 100 employees, the plant in 1967 was staffed by only ten. It was bought in 1974 by the New Jersey Department of Environmental Protection for $100, part of 4,670 acres purchased with money from Federal Aid to Wildlife. The money was raised by a tax on hunting equipment. Now a Wildlife Management Area, the island is used for bird watching, salt water fishing, crabbing, and water fowl hunting.

The factory's remains have not been removed. The state seems to be considering several plans: to reclaim the area

and turn it back into tidal marsh. In 1982, a fire at the factory may have been deliberately set. An investigation found small amounts of asbestos, whose removal would add to the cost of reclamation—in excess of a million dollars. Under state regulation, the structures cannot be buried there but would have to go to a landfill. Another proposal was to use the heavy metal and concrete for an artificial reef.

The Crab Island ruins tell a rich story of American industrialized fishing between 1850 and 1974. Preservationists hope that the state of New Jersey will be able to retain some of the derelict buildings to help us remember and permit us to reflect on our industrial past.

Notes

1. I am grateful to the Tuckerton, NJ, Historical Society for sharing newspaper clippings and early photographs of the Crab Island factory with me. Without Lori Edmunds' most interesting article, *The Stinkhouse on Crab Island* (Tuckerton Historical Society Newsletter, Oct. 2008), this chapter could not have been written. Edmunds includes her own reminiscences of a visit to Crab Island and invaluable information from the following people who had a direct connection to the factory: A. Shell, Figley, J. Siegfried, C. Stocker, H. Heinrich, Jasinski, Soldwedel, R. Haul, Widjeskog, and B.Haul.
2. N.J. Mirror 6/10/1885
3. N.J. Mirror, Tuckerton Section 7/29/1885
4. W. Ross Yates, *Joseph Wharton: Quaker Industrial Pioneer* (Bethlehem, PA: Lehigh University Press, 1987).
5. John Frye, *The Men All Singing: The Story of Menhaden Fishing* (Virginia Beach, VA: The Donning Company, 1978).

Contributors' Biographies

Ruth Formanek, photographer and psychologist, has been a keen observer of nature and human behavior since childhood. A professional photographer, Formanek has had several solo exhibitions and often participates in group shows. A clinical psychologist with a post-doctoral degree in Psychotherapy and Psychoanalysis from Adelphi University, she is Professor emerita at Hofstra University where she taught Child Development for over 30 years. During that time she was active in research projects, and wrote and edited books on children's and women's cognitive and clinical issues. Formanek lived in Amagansett for 25 years where she discovered the Walking Dunes and the Hicks Island fish factory ruins to be a photographer's dream. Currently a member of the Park West Camera Club and the Soho Photo Gallery in Manhattan, she has won awards for her work. She has recently presented papers about the connections between psychology and photography at annual meetings of the American Psychological Association. Formanek has traveled extensively and, in addition to her digital portfolio of Atlantic Coast fish factories and the Walking Dunes, she has photographed Anasazi ruins in the West and old Jewish cemeteries in Germany.

H. Bruce Franklin is one of America's leading cultural historians. He has published or edited nineteen books and hundreds of articles on American history, literature and culture. He has taught at Stanford, Yale, Johns Hopkins and Wesleyan, and is currently the John Cotton Dana Professor of English and American Studies at Rutgers University in Newark. Before Franklin got his doctorate, he flew for three years as a navigator and intelligence officer in the Strategic Air Command. His love of the sea has been lifelong. As a teenager he worked briefly as a mate on a fishing boat. Later he worked in New York Harbor as a deckhand and mate on tugboats, including some of the last steam tugboats. He is a past President of the Herman Melville Society. Bruce Franklin is also an avid fisherman, which led him to his current concern with menhaden and their relation to the marine environment. His influential 2001 article about menhaden in *Discover* magazine was included in that year's *The Best American Science and Nature Writing*. His 2007 book, *The Most Important Fish in the Sea,* shows that menhaden not only play crucial roles in our marine environment but also have been an important part of American history from the seventeenth century right through our current crisis.

William Wise: For the past 23 years, William Wise has been the Associate Director of Stony Brook University's School of Marine and Atmospheric Sciences. He also directs the School's Living Marine Resources Institute (or LMRI). Prior to coming to Stony Brook, Wise was the Assistant and then Acting-Director of the New York Sea Grant Program, then headquartered in Albany, New York. His interests and expertise include fisheries and fisheries management, marine policy, aquaculture and marine education. Wise chairs a number of governmental and non-governmental bodies that advise on priority regional marine resource management issues, including the New York State Marine Resources Advisory Council, the Surf Clam/ Ocean Quahog Management Advisory Board, and The Nature Conservancy's Bluepoints Bottomlands Council. Among other involvements, he is a trustee of The Long Island Chapter of The Nature Conservancy.